T0052206

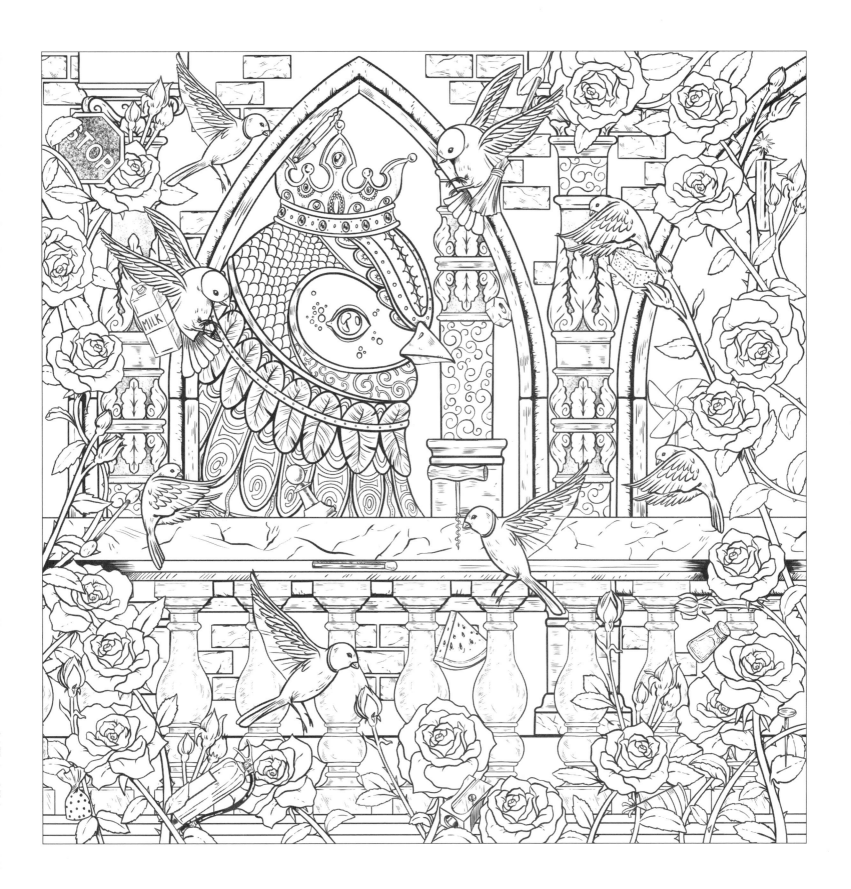

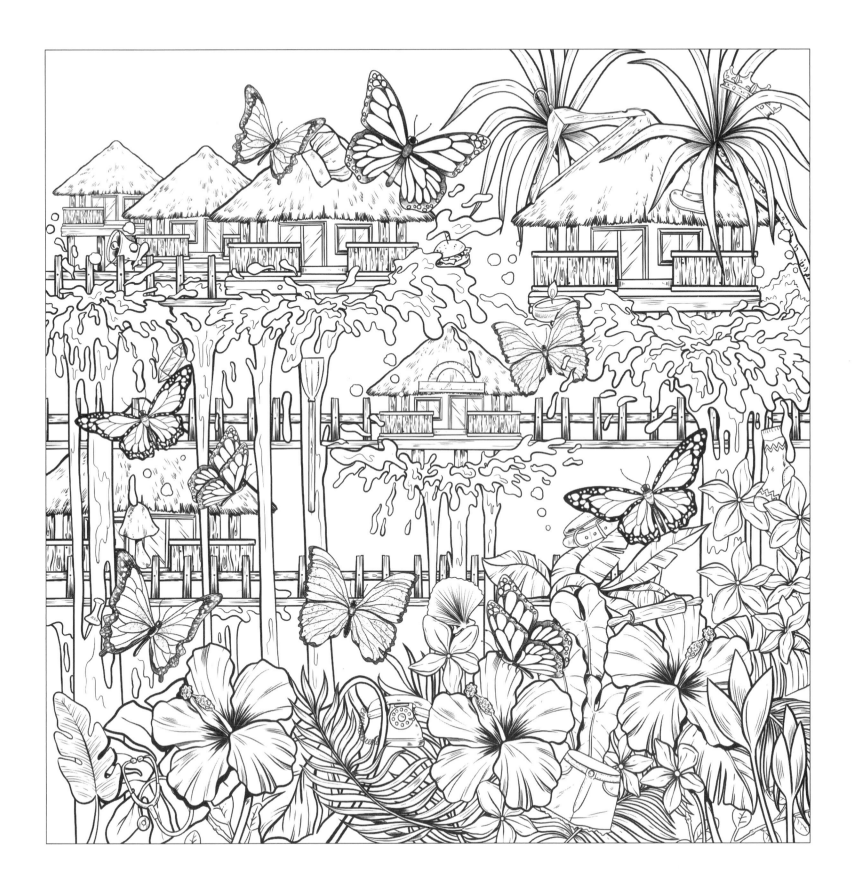

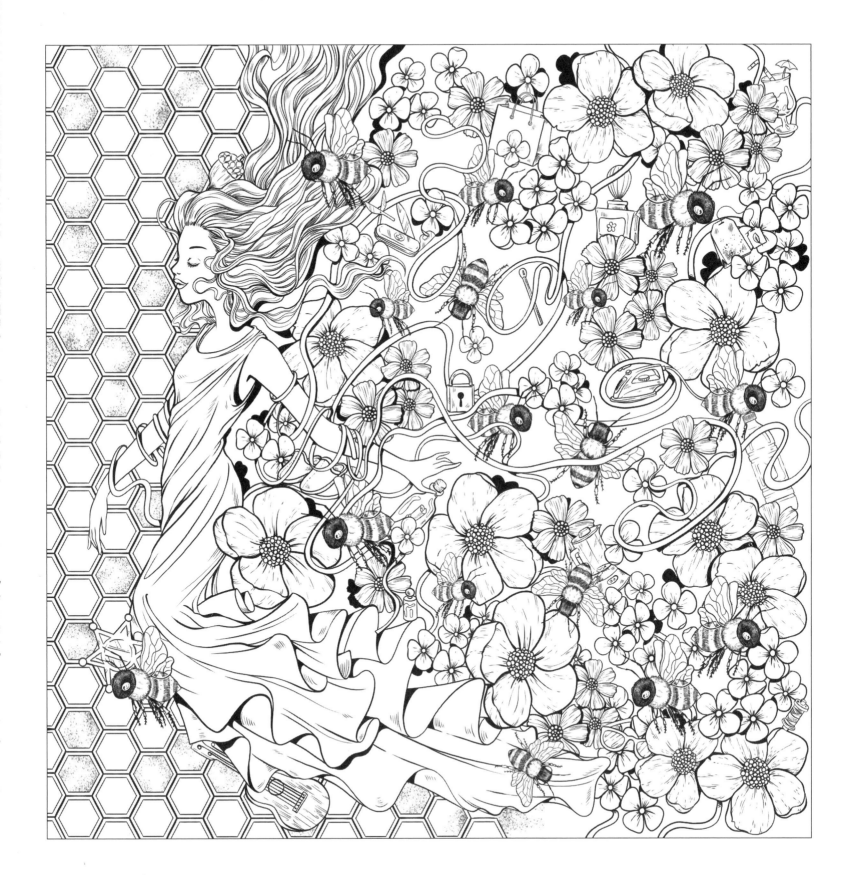

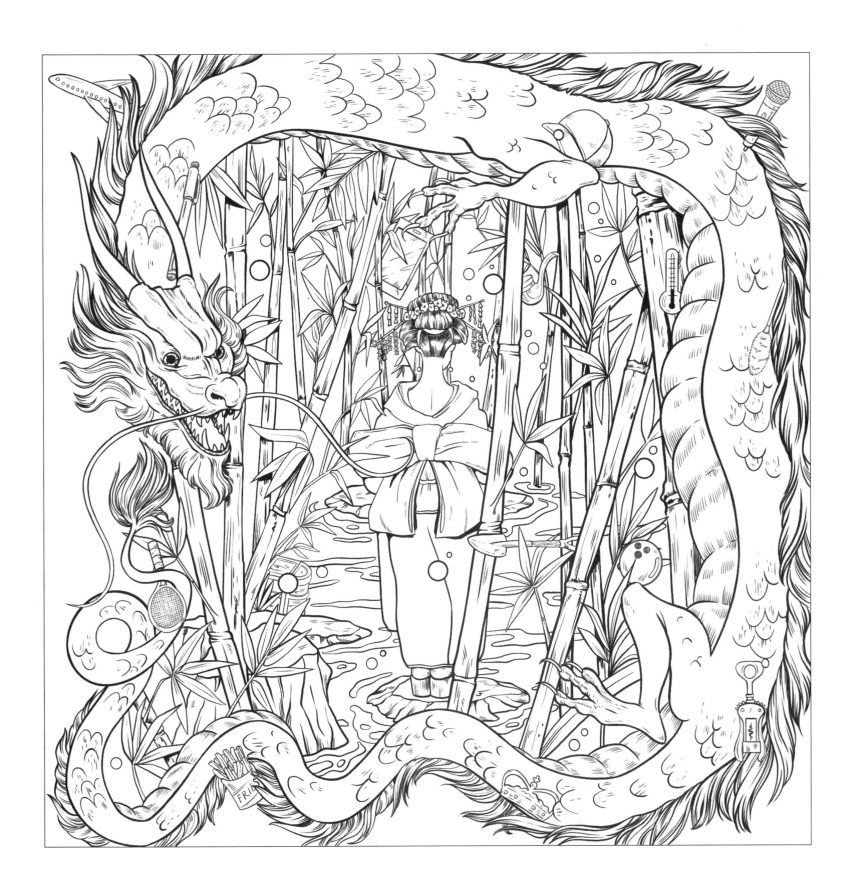

HIDDEN OBJECTS REVEALED

COVER

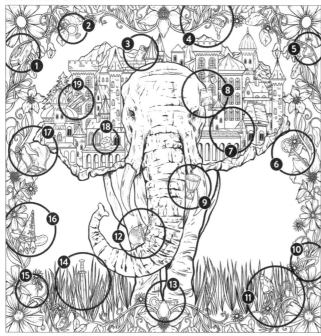

1. Telescope 2. Bell 3. Screw 4. Lightbulb 5. Hourglass
6. Rubik's Cube 7. Horseshoe 8. Paper Boat 9. Trophy
10. Tube of Paint 11. Ice Cream Pop 12. Skeleton Key

DOLPHIN

1. Makeup Brush 2. Bow and Arrow 3. Map 4. Calculator 5. Comb
6. Firework 7. Musical Note 8. Ball Mask 9. Sack of Gold
10. Coffee Cup 11. Erlenmeyer Flask 12. Ice Cream Pop 13. Wrench
14. Padlock 15. Arrow

ELEPHANT CITY

1. Tissues 2. Diamond Ring 3. Lighter 4. Honey Stirrer
5. Erlenmeyer Flask 6. Magic Wand 7. Pickaxe 8. Tea Bag 9. Bongo
10. Carabiner 11. Stone Spear 12. Coconut Drink 13. Skeleton Key
14. Sword 15. Sack 16. Witch's Hat 17. Paper Lantern 18. Bolt 19. Cutlery

WISTERIA GIRL

1. Saw 2. Speech Bubble 3. Pizza Cutter 4. Popcorn 5. Pencil
6. Theater Masks 7. Clog 8. Cola 9. Screwdriver 10. Snowflake
11. Brush 12. Trophy 13. Parchment 14. Oven Mitt 15. Die

SWAN LAKE

1 Button **2** Poker Club **3** Music Note **4** Perfume **5** Camera
6 Crystal Necklace **7** Pear **8** Gloves **9** Cupid's Heart
10 Spray Cleaner **11** Play Button **12** Safety Pin **13** Salt Shaker
14 Bone **15** Anchor **16** Ticket **17** Candy **18** Earring

GALAXY

1 Lightbulb **2** Paintbrush **3** Skeleton Key **4** Jar **5** Lollipop
6 Gear **7** Desk Lamp **8** Pencil **9** Telephone **10** Padlock
11 Briefcase **12** Jump Rope **13** Paper Boat **14** Ice Cream Cone **15** Book
16 Ice Skates **17** Toothpaste

RAINBOW WATERFALL

1 Rubber Ducky **2** Lemon Slice **3** Sack of Gold **4** Razor
5 Playing Card **6** Die **7** Billiard Ball **8** Soap Dispenser
9 Hairbrush **10** Car **11** Hammer **12** Cork **13** Pocket Mirror
14 Compass **15** Hairdryer

QUEEN OF THE BIRDS

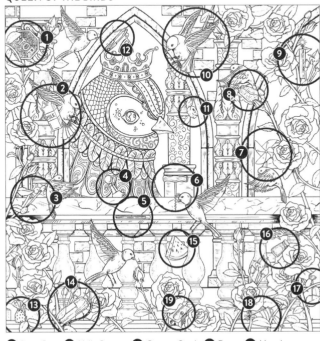

1 Stop Sign **2** Milk Carton **3** Cotton Swab **4** Pawn **5** Match
6 Corkscrew **7** Pinwheel **8** Sponge **9** Dynamite **10** Broom **11** Bolt
12 Kitchen Tongs **13** Candy **14** Fire Extinguisher **15** Watermelon Slice
16 Salt Shaker **17** Nail **18** Birthday Hat **19** Pencil Sharpener

SUNFLOWER

1 Balloon 2 Knife 3 Bowling Pin 4 Razor 5 Set Square
6 Poker Chip 7 Drink 8 Pencil 9 Magnifying Glass 10 Gift
11 Lemon 12 Lipstick 13 Spool of Thread 14 Party Hat
15 Pizza 16 Diamond

WINDMILL

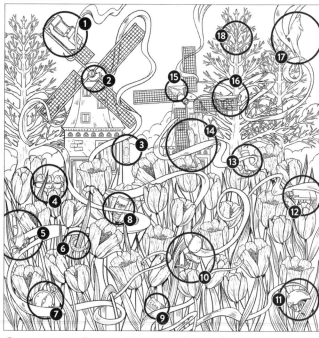

1 Arcade Game 2 Arrow 3 Bandage 4 Eggs 5 Magic Lamp
6 Horseshoe 7 Compass 8 Cream 9 Credit Card 10 Office Chair
11 Helmet 12 Flash Drive 13 Rainboot 14 Pepper 15 Paper Airplane
16 Axe 17 Dolphin 18 Scissors

KOI

1 Rainboot 2 Balloon 3 Party Garland 4 Hanger 5 Feather
6 Magic Wand 7 Love Letter 8 Candle 9 Thimble 10 Accordion
11 Gift 12 Drink 13 Crown 14 Cherries 15 Candy 16 Whistle 17 Zipper
18 Shuttlecock 19 Croissant 20 Diamond

BUTTERFLY PARADISE

1 Chef's Hat 2 Bell 3 Crystal 4 Mushroom 5 Oar 6 Protractor
7 Tack 8 Stethoscope 9 Telephone 10 Shorts 11 Rolling Pin 12 Belt
13 Sock 14 Candle 15 Hamburger 16 Hanger 17 Witch's Hat 18 Crown

LOVE BIRDS

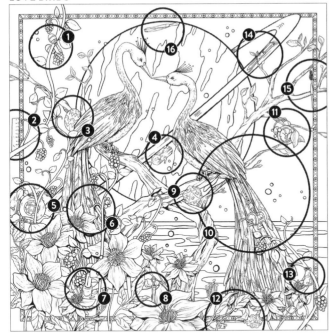

1 Maracas 2 Ruler 3 Easter Egg 4 Log 5 Diver's Helmet
6 Makeup Brush 7 Nail Polish 8 Stone Ax 9 RPG Die
10 Fishing Pole 11 Alarm Clock 12 Skeleton Key 13 Erlenmeyer Flask
14 Pen 15 Mascara Brush 16 Tweezers

SURF

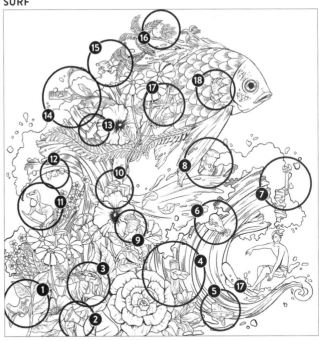

1 Cowboy Boot 2 Megaphone 3 Power Drill 4 Rolling Pin
5 Cooking Pot 6 Sack of Gold 7 Wrench 8 Oil Drum 9 Lemonade
10 Toy Blocks 11 Rocking Horse 12 Candy 13 Arrow 14 Comb
15 Bow 16 Potted Plant 17 Pickaxe 18 Medieval Helmet

WINGS

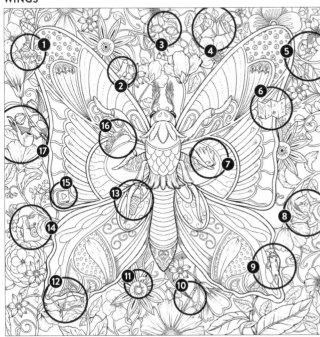

1 Ornament 2 Sock 3 Eyeglasses 4 Megaphone 5 Fork
6 Map 7 Gloves 8 Cola 9 Candle 10 Pen 11 Musical Note
12 Bow and Arrow 13 Ice Cream Cone 14 T-Shirt 15 Play Button
16 Taco 17 Smoking Pipe

WOLF SONG

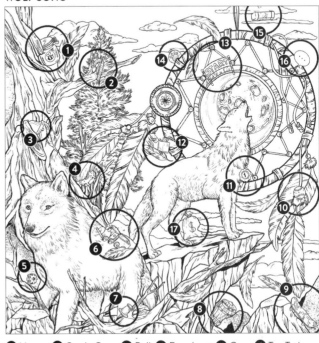

1 Honey 2 Candy Cane 3 Bell 4 Doughnut 5 Gear 6 Toy Train
7 Tack 8 Barrel 9 Skateboard 10 Baseball 11 1st Place Sash 12 Lighter
13 Start Banner 14 Dog Tag 15 Eraser 16 Speech Bubble 17 Sack of Gold

CHERRY BLOSSOM

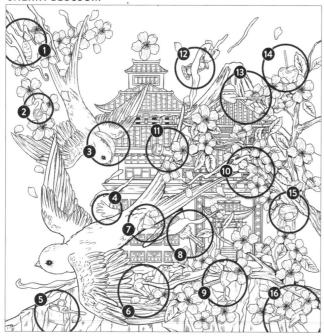

1 Duster 2 Do-Not-Disturb Tag 3 Banana 4 Glove 5 Shopping Bag
6 Lightbulb 7 Baseball Cap 8 Key 9 Wine Glass 10 Smoking Pipe
11 Flashlight 12 Hourglass 13 Shovel 14 Caramel Apple
15 Wooden Stool 16 Trowel

MOTHER NATURE

1 Slippers 2 Soccer Ball 3 Pen 4 Tack 5 Box Cutter
6 Pencil Sharpener 7 Lemon Slice 8 Boot 9 Sack of Diamonds
10 Trophy 11 Comb 12 Juice 13 Kite 14 Potion Bottle
15 Teacup 16 Ball of Yarn

FLAMINGO

1 Dessert 2 Calendar 3 Lighter 4 Sunglasses 5 Oven Mitt
6 Lipstick 7 Watering Can 8 Broom 9 Rolling Pin 10 Tack
11 Parchment 12 Hairbrush 13 Soccer Ball 14 Smoking Pipe
15 MP3 Player 16 Game Controller

MAGIC LAKE

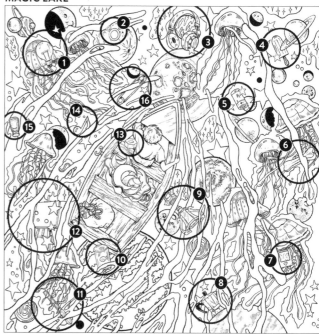

1 Light Bulb 2 Diamond Ring 3 Headphones 4 Ice Cream Pop
5 Battery 6 Dog Bone 7 Photo 8 Espresso Pot 9 Trophy
10 Tin Fish 11 Grater 12 Canvas 13 Bolt 14 Music Note
15 Salt Shaker 16 Safety Pin

TURTLE

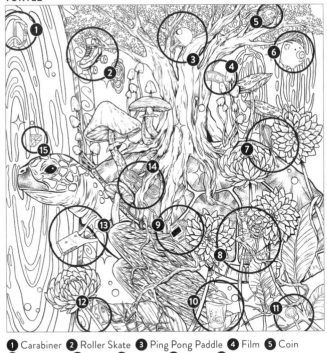

1 Carabiner **2** Roller Skate **3** Ping Pong Paddle **4** Film **5** Coin
6 Piggy Bank **7** Whisk **8** Hookah **9** Watch **10** Drink
11 Magnifying Glass **12** Can of Tuna **13** Industrial Stapler
14 Rope **15** Diamond

CRYSTAL UNICORN

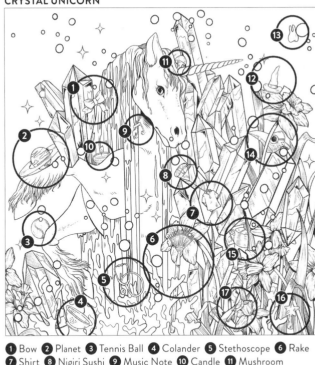

1 Bow **2** Planet **3** Tennis Ball **4** Colander **5** Stethoscope **6** Rake
7 Shirt **8** Nigiri Sushi **9** Music Note **10** Candle **11** Mushroom
12 Witch's Hat **13** Tooth **14** Plague Mask **15** Cooking Pot
16 Christmas Tree Star **17** Pruning Shears

TIME

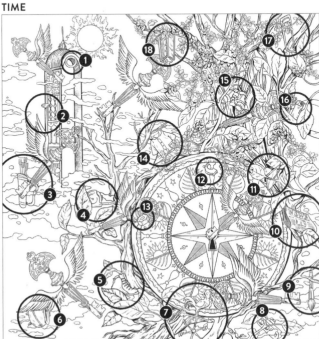

1 Diamond Ring **2** Nail **3** Quiver **4** Tape Measure **5** Shoe
6 Cauldron **7** Weather Vane **8** Power Strip **9** Makeup Brush
10 Newspaper **11** Graduation Cap **12** Arrow **13** Bolt **14** Coat
15 Binoculars **16** Lighter **17** Saw **18** Makeup Palette

GRAMOPHONE

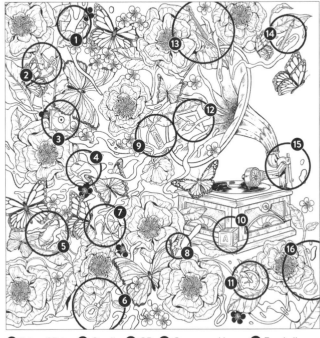

1 Tube of Paint **2** Candle **3** CD **4** Computer Mouse **5** Football
6 Magnifying Glass **7** Flip-Flops **8** Tack **9** Crayon **10** Toy Block
11 Alarm Clock **12** Set Square **13** Violin **14** Pencil **15** Compass **16** Ladle

REFLECTION

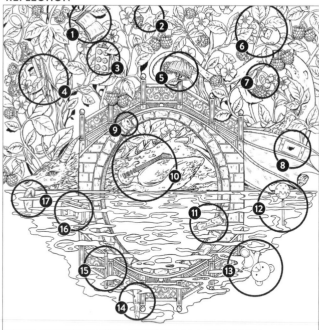

1 Book **2** Star **3** Toy Brick **4** Hair Straightener **5** Wicker Basket
6 Kokeshi Doll **7** Soap Bottle **8** Cell Phone **9** Bolt **10** Electric Guitar
11 Toothpaste **12** Lollipop **13** Teddy Bear **14** Lipstick **15** Pencil
16 Alarm Clock **17** Flip-Flop

QUEEN BEE

1 Acorn **2** Swiss Army Knife **3** Shopping Bag **4** Perfume
5 Umbrella Drink **6** Tea Bag **7** Match **8** Iron **9** Plastic Bottle
10 Spool of Thread **11** Sunglasses **12** Mini Bottle **13** Blender
14 Message in a Bottle **15** Slippers **16** Padlock **17** Sheriff's Badge **18** Guitar

PEACEFUL

1 Tack **2** Doughnut **3** Puzzle Piece **4** Briefcase **5** Question Mark
6 Crayon **7** Bell **8** Watch **9** Shopping Cart **10** Scrub Brush
11 Wallet **12** Spoon **13** Set Square **14** Pacifier **15** Fan **16** Ink Bottle
17 Hammer **18** Crystal Ball **19** Chandelier **20** Painting Set

SNOWGLOBE

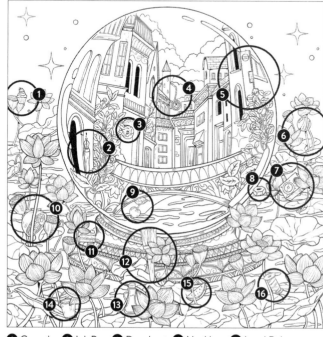

1 Cupcake **2** Ink Pen **3** Doughnut **4** Necklace **5** Level Ruler
6 Lollipop **7** Speaker **8** Bolt **9** Cherry **10** Ramen Bowl
11 Slice of Cake **12** Brush **13** Oil Bottle **14** Bucket
15 Watermelon Slice **16** Spool of Thread

SWEET PARADISE

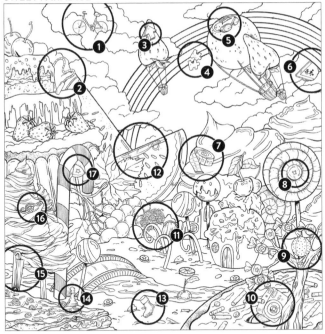

1 Bicycle 2 Jump Rope 3 Arrow Icon 4 Puzzle Pieces
5 Swimming Goggles 6 Pedestrian Sign 7 Measuring Tape 8 Button
9 Hot Air Balloon 10 Camera 11 Bouquet of Roses 12 Sword
13 Rainboot 14 Chess Piece 15 Umbrella 16 Treble Clef 17 Baseball Cap

WONDERLAND

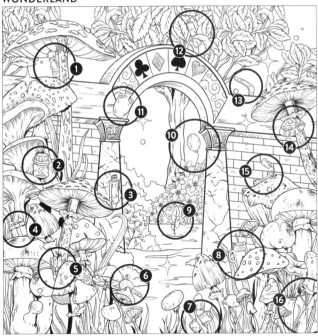

1 Pepper Grinder 2 Vitamin Bottle 3 Flash Drive 4 Gift
5 Shuttlecock 6 Ping Pong Paddle 7 Soda Can 8 Juice 9 Feather
10 Balloon 11 Ancient Pot 12 Tube of Paint 13 Boomerang 14 Dog Bowl
15 Room Key 16 Sushi

BOOK CITY

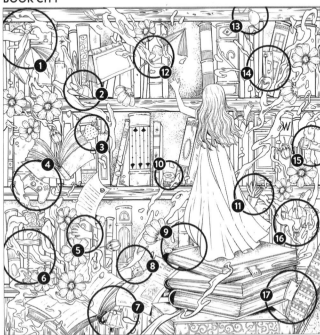

1 Tie 2 Baseball Cap 3 Strawberry 4 Game Controller 5 Glove
6 Corkscrew 7 Espresso Pot 8 Battery 9 Cotton Swab 10 Bolt
11 Plant 12 Smoking Pipe 13 Balloon 14 Suitcase 15 Flashlight
16 Hot Air Balloon 17 Butcher's Knife

LANTERNS

1 Beach Ball 2 Music Note 3 Protractor 4 Painting 5 Lighter
6 Salt Shaker 7 Watering Can 8 2nd Place Sash 9 Lollipop
10 Dynamite 11 Pin 12 Sailor Hat 13 Microphone
14 Target 15 Sunglasses

UNDER THE SEA

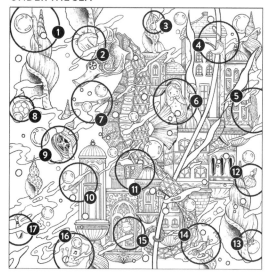

1 Pepper 2 Baseball Glove 3 Music Note
4 Moon Pendant 5 Ear of Corn 6 Nesting Doll
7 Fork 8 Soccer Ball 9 Film Reel 10 Scissors
11 Calculator 12 Perfume 13 Tomato 14 Magic Lamp
15 Glass of Wine 16 MP3 Player 17 Bowling Pin

BEACH

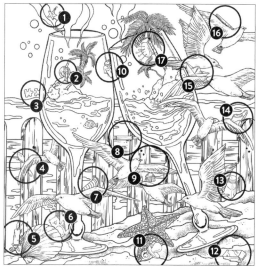

1 Star Pendant 2 Button 3 Puzzle Pieces 4 Spoon
5 Candle 6 Teddy Bear 7 Traffic Cone 8 Crayon
9 Broom 10 Shirt 11 Pacifier 12 Milk Carton 13 Bottle
14 Shoe 15 Paper Boat 16 Pen 17 Pin Cushion

PYRAMID OASIS

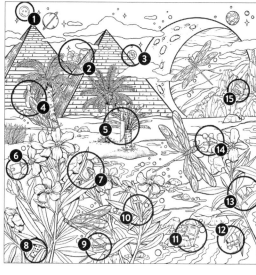

1 Button 2 Yarn 3 Poker Chip 4 Bowling Pin
5 Kitchen Knife 6 Wallet 7 Scuba Goggles
8 Domino Piece 9 Hamburger 10 Hammer
11 Game Boy 12 Gift 13 Flag 14 Cherries 15 Credit Card

FORBIDDEN CITY

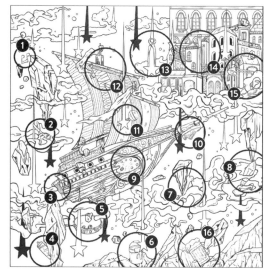

1 Music Note 2 Scissors 3 Screw 4 Spray Paint
5 Tambourine 6 Paint 7 Bone 8 Lightbulb 9 Palette
10 Athletic Shoe 11 Lollipop 12 Pencil 13 Tongs 14 Brush
15 Desk Lamp 16 Beer

CAROUSEL

1 Paper Airplane 2 Electric Toothbrush 3 Fork
4 Pen 5 Hourglass 6 Pill Bottle 7 Scarf
8 Padlock 9 Puzzle Piece 10 Fan 11 Tweezers
12 Skeleton Key 13 Parchment

DRAGON

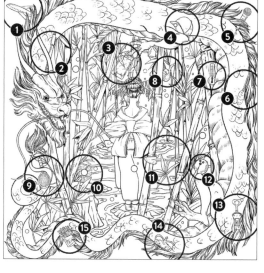

1 Airplane 2 Ballpoint Pen 3 Tablet 4 Baseball Cap
5 Microphone 6 Duster 7 Thermometer
8 Smoking Pipe 9 Tennis Racket 10 Trunk 11 Shovel
12 Bowling Ball 13 Corkscrew 14 Crown 15 Fries

LIGHTHOUSE

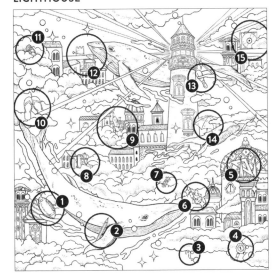

1 Football 2 Pencil 3 Question Mark 4 1ˢᵗ Place Sash
5 Set Square 6 Bell 7 Spool of Thread 8 Paint Roller
9 Candle 10 Flip-Flop 11 Ring 12 Oar 13 Bowling Pin
14 Umbrella 15 CD

FOUNTAIN

1 Jet 2 Music Note 3 Scissors 4 Chess Piece
5 Watermelon Slice 6 Horseshoe 7 Bandage
8 Screw 9 Umbrella 10 Paper Clip 11 Diploma
12 Magnifying Glass 13 Ink Pen 14 Cash 15 Brush
16 Necklace 17 Die 18 Four-Leaf Clover

PASSION FLOWER

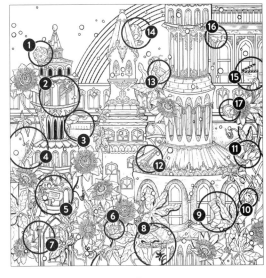

1 RPG Die 2 Toothbrush 3 Ruler 4 Fishhook
5 Key Tag 6 Diamond 7 Nail 8 Chain 9 Sock
10 Bolt 11 Bottle 12 Scissors 13 Spice Shaker 14 Globe
15 Clapperboard 16 Paper Airplane 17 Poker Chip

ANCHOR

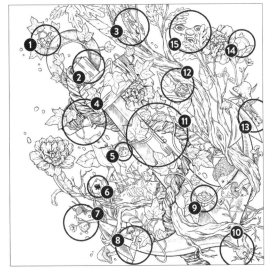

1 Bow 2 Lighter 3 Athletic Shoe 4 Plug 5 Die
6 Poker Card 7 Perfume 8 Lipstick 9 Toy Brick
10 Key 11 Fork 12 Paint Brush 13 Clothespin
14 Ornament 15 Fidget Spinner

FLYING FISH

1 Baseball Cap 2 Screw 3 Domino Piece 4 Cauldron
5 Sword 6 Box of Chocolates 7 Mouthwash
8 Toothbrush 9 Fork 10 Pen 11 Videogame Mushroom
12 Quiver 13 Hair Clip 14 Button 15 Bolt

Discover more of Mythographic

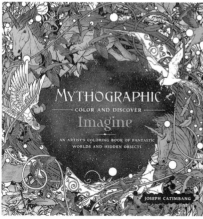
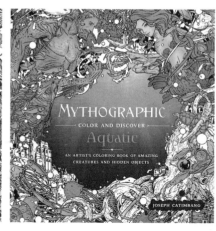

MYTHOGRAPHIC COLOR AND DISCOVER: PARADISE.

Copyright © 2020 by St. Martin's Press.

All rights reserved. Printed in Canada. For information,

address St. Martin's Press, 120 Broadway, New York, NY 10271.

www.castlepointbooks.com

The Castle Point Books trademark is owned by Castle Point Publishing, LLC.

Castle Point books are published and distributed by St. Martin's Press.

ISBN 978-1-250-27040-5 (trade paperback)

Cover design by Young Lim

Edited by Monica Sweeney

Our books may be purchased in bulk for promotional, educational, or business use.

Please contact your local bookseller or the Macmillan Corporate

and Premium Sales Department at 1-800-221-7945, extension 5442,

or by email at MacmillanSpecialMarkets@macmillan.com.

First Edition: 2020

10 9 8 7 6 5 4 3 2